■ ORGANIZATIONS ■
THAT HELP THE WORLD

GREENPEACE

PAUL BROWN

Picture credits:
Jacana Ann Ronan at Image Select, Greenpeace Communications, Gamma

The Publishers would like to extend a special thanks to John
May through acknowledging their indebtedness to his
extensive original work in his books *The Greenpeace
Story,* written with Michael Brown (Dorling Kindersley,
1991), and *The Greenpeace Book of Antarctica* (Dorling
Kindersley, 1989).

Published in Great Britain in 1993
by Exley Publications Ltd,
16 Chalk Hill, Watford,
Herts WD1 4BN, United Kingdom.

Copyright © Exley Publications, 1993
Text copyright © Paul Brown, 1993

**A copy of the CIP data is available from
the British Library on request.**

ISBN 1-85015-366-3

Series editor: Helen Exley
Editor: Samantha Armstrong
Editorial Assistant: Helen Lanz
Research: Margaret Montgomery
Picture research: Alex Goldberg and James
Clift of Image Select
Typeset by Delta Print, Watford, Herts, UK
Printed by Kultura, Budapest

GREENPEACE

PAUL BROWN

Stop the bomb!

On September 15, 1971 twelve Canadian volunteers set sail in an old fishing boat from Vancouver on Canada's west coast to try and stop a nuclear bomb being exploded. No one had ever taken such a risk before: if they sailed too close to where the bomb was to be let off, they could be blown to pieces.

Even though they were frightened, they went because the Americans would not listen to their demands that the test should not be allowed. The volunteers believed that the bomb could damage a wildlife haven, cause an earthquake and even create a tidal wave. They hoped that they would be able to reach the test site, anchor their boat in the danger zone and stop the planned explosion. Among the volunteers were journalists, who would send daily reports to their newspapers and radio stations so that the authorities would know where they were. The protesters gambled that the military would not be prepared to let the bomb off and risk killing them and face the bad publicity it would cause.

Don't make a wave

This voyage was the birth of Greenpeace. Originally part of a protest group called the "Don't Make a Wave Committee", the campaigners realized it was not a very catchy name. They looked for another and came up with "Greenpeace", combining the "green" of the environment campaigners, and the "peace" of those against nuclear weapons. In just twenty years, the Greenpeace organization would grow to have offices in thirty countries, more than six ships and more than four million members worldwide.

It spread from North America to New Zealand,

Opposite: Eleven million tons of the powerful explosive, TNT, form a sinister mushroom cloud, as the Americans stage another nuclear test in the Pacific. Some of the surrounding islands are made uninhabitable due to radioactive fallout. Greenpeace grew from the demonstrations to stop these tests.

"Today...Greenpeace is working right around the world to save rainforests, avert global warming, oppose toxic pollution and confront nuclear folly."

*From "Actions Speak Louder",
a Greenpeace publication, 1993.*

5

The Canadian volunteers prepare their boat, the "Phyllis Cormack", for their voyage of protest – the first of its kind – to make the government listen to their fears concerning the dangers of nuclear testing.

Australia and to Europe. It now has offices in South America and Russia. Greenpeace campaigns concentrate on stopping pollution and saving wildlife from needless destruction. As in the first voyage, protesters often sail into forbidden military areas and face arrest or being shot. In other campaigns, they put their bodies between a harpoon and a whale, or risk contamination when blocking a toxic or radioactive waste pipe.

To Amchitka

In this first protest the Greenpeace pioneers were concerned because a serious earthquake, in the same area as the proposed bomb tests, had caused tidal waves along the coasts of Alaska and Canada and as far away as Japan.

Their protest boat, the *Phyllis Cormack,* was renamed the *Greenpeace* for this first voyage. For fifteen days the crew battled against terrible weather as they headed for the test site. This was on a small, American-owned island called Amchitka, close to the Arctic Circle, off the north-west coast of Alaska. The boat's engine broke down on the second day and had to be repaired at sea, the compass did not work properly, and many of the crew were seasick, but the expedition continued on its two-thousand-mile voyage.

When their fuel and food began to run low, the crew asked a US navy base they passed for help – but were refused. Despite this, the crew decided to continue on their mission and put in at the island of Akutan before sailing on.

They had not got very far when their boat was chased by the US coastguard and arrested, being forced to sail back many miles to complete customs forms.

These official obstructions, the poor condition of the boat, and the worsening weather exhausted the twelve pioneers as they pushed on to the test site. They had been twenty-seven days at sea. The waves, crashing on the deck, began to turn to ice as the winter approached. The crew knew they might have to last another month before the bomb test. Some felt it was too dangerous to continue and others, who had taken time off from work to be on board, feared they might lose their jobs. After a long argument, the crew voted by eight to four to turn back.

Warriors of the Rainbow

Sadly, they sailed home, thinking themselves failures, and believing they had wasted the donations of hundreds of people who had given money to their cause. To their surprise, the people of Canada did not agree.

On their way home, the *Greenpeace* called at Kodiak Island, off Alaska, where the city council gave the crew a banquet to celebrate their bravery. At Alert Bay, forty Kwatkiutl Indians met them and at a ceremony made them blood brothers of the people. It was to be the beginning of a special relationship with the Indians.

The Indian people told them of a two-hundred-year-old prophesy made by an old Cree Indian woman, Eyes of Fire. She had said there would come a time when the earth would be ravaged of its resources, the sea blackened, the streams poisoned, the deer dropping dead in their tracks. Just before it was too late, the Indian people would regain their spirit and teach the white people reverence for the earth, banding together to become Warriors of the Rainbow and save the world.

"Great are the tasks ahead, terrifying are the mountains of ignorance and hate and prejudice, but the Warriors of the Rainbow shall rise as on the wings of the eagle to surmount all difficulties."

Willoya and Brown, from "Warriors of the Rainbow".

The crew of the "Phyllis Cormack" carry out their protest actions to stop nuclear testing. Greenpeace is against nuclear testing because of the harmful effects it has on both humans and the environment. Radiation, from nuclear explosions, can cause severe illness and destroy wildlife.

7

Relieved to be back safely, the first Greenpeace crew, on the "Phyllis Cormack", are surprised to return to growing public support for their mission to prevent the US nuclear testing at Amchitka, in 1971.

"Non-violent direct action is our unique way of exposing environmental crime. It creates headline news. And makes guilty parties clean up their act, under heavy public pressure."

From "Actions Speak Louder", a Greenpeace publication, 1993.

Success

The journalists' reports of the protesters' journey, the obstruction by the military when they needed help, and the arrest of the ship and crew had aroused public sympathy. While they were away, more money had been collected and a much larger ship had been chartered to replace their tiny vessel. Four hundred people had volunteered to act as the crew, although only twenty-eight were needed. Even before the *Greenpeace* had returned home, the second ship had set off to take its place.

The second ship was renamed *Greenpeace Too* for its voyage. Bad weather and the huge distance to cover meant the new ship was still seven hundred miles short of the test zone when the bomb was let off. The explosion was measured in Canada as the same size as a large earthquake... but the worst fears of the protesters were not realized. Despite the terrible vibrations deep in the earth, the nuclear bomb did not trigger further tremors nor create the tidal wave that some scientists had predicted.

Instead, the American government faced a tidal wave of protests from people all over Canada and America about the use of the island for tests. Within a few days, the United States Atomic Energy Commission, surprised by the strength of feeling, announced that there would be no more tests on the island that year. Three months later, the Commission officially abandoned Amchitka Island as a testing ground for "political and other reasons" and turned it into a bird sanctuary.

It was the first time that a public protest of that kind had affected official policy. Without realizing it, those first twelve volunteers had created a blueprint for dozens of future protests. They had laid the foundations of Greenpeace – a new style environmental group that was to attract sympathizers from around the world. They had shown that a tiny boat, pitted against the might of the authorities, gained public sympathy, a modern version of the David and Goliath story in the Bible.

An important trick

Some of the early members of Greenpeace were Quakers, a religious group who believe in non-violent protest, what they call "bearing witness". This often means going to where people are being tortured or wrongly imprisoned and maintaining a vigil to show disapproval. The twelve crew of the *Greenpeace* had begun this silent protest, or non-violent direct action. It became the trademark of the Greenpeace organization.

As in the first protest, this often meant putting a boat and the lives of the crew at risk by sailing into a nuclear test zone or similar forbidden area. But the most important trick that Greenpeace learned was *always* to have a reporter and, even more important, someone with a camera on hand. This way, every time the technique of direct action was used, television viewers across the world could see volunteers in action. Sometimes they would be climbing factory chimneys to hang banners, sometimes wading up to their necks in the sea to block waste pipes, and, perhaps the most dazzling, campaigners in fast rubber dinghies racing in front of whaling boats and placing their bodies in the path of the harpoons. These exploits brought in thousands of new members.

A Greenpeace protester literally gets it in the neck, as he climbs up the side of the "Pacific Sandpiper" – a cargo vessel, transporting spent nuclear fuel from Japan to Sellafield, in the UK. Here, uranium and plutonium are extracted to be re-used; the remaining nuclear waste is either stored or dumped at sea. Nuclear waste can remain radioactive, and therefore harmful, for thousands of years.

The organization had only been formed in 1971 to campaign about one set of nuclear bomb tests. Once that threat had lifted, the infant organization might have just as quickly faded away again.

But in another part of the world, thousands of miles away in the South Pacific, more nuclear tests were planned. This time they were to be carried out by a different country, France.

A special kind of spirit

In Canada, the Greenpeace Foundation, which had collected money to protest about the first tests, had no idea if there was anything they could do about this new series. But they did have some money left. They could see that it was too far to sail all the way from Canada to the South Pacific in a small boat and try the same tactics again. So they decided to advertise for volunteers in the nearest country to the test site.

In New Zealand, the advertisement was seen by a former Canadian badminton champion and business executive, David McTaggart, who had given up his previous life to sail around the Pacific. McTaggart had never really thought about nuclear testing, but was angry that France had decided to create a two-hundred-mile exclusion zone which, in effect, meant cordoning off 100,000 square miles of ocean to blow up these bombs. He believed this decision was contrary to international law and the historic rights of freedom of navigation enjoyed by all people for centuries.

With the aid of some money from the Greenpeace Foundation, McTaggart and other volunteers prepared his yacht, *Vega,* for the long voyage to the French test site. It would mean many weeks at sea but, as before, there was no shortage of people who shared the outrage at the proposed bomb tests and were prepared to risk their lives. Later, describing these events, McTaggart remembered something unusual about those who came forward. They were a different kind of person to those he had known before, with a special kind of spirit. There was a different atmosphere on the boat than the "competitive, raucous" crowd he had known in business. The volunteers showed up quietly by the

Main picture: David McTaggart's own yacht, the "Vega", was renamed "Greenpeace III" for the voyage to Moruroa. It was equipped by Greenpeace with a new inflatable life-raft and a long-range radio transceiver, ready for the seven-thousand-mile round trip to the Pacific island where the French navy planned to carry out further nuclear testing.

score. Each one of them seizing on any task, however difficult or dirty, and applying themselves vigorously for many hours without complaint.

Moruroa

The French test site at Moruroa was a daunting 3,500 miles away. This was far more dangerous even than the first voyage, partly because of the vast distance involved in an even smaller boat, and the fact that the bombs were to be blown up in the air rather than underground. This meant the yacht and the crew of *Vega* could be destroyed and killed, if they were too close to the bombs when they were exploded. Anywhere closer than one hundred miles and they would be at risk from radioactive fallout.

As a symbol of peace, the dove is adopted as a Greenpeace motif.

Just before the boat left at the end of April 1972 *Vega* had the name *Greenpeace III* sewn into its sail. It was May 31 before McTaggart and his two crew reached their target. The *Vega* finally entered the two-hundred-mile zone around Moruroa, the area from which the French had banned all ships.

On board the yacht, McTaggart had a carefully drawn up document from the University of Auckland. It showed that the rules about the two-hundred-mile exclusion zone the French had invented were illegal. Under the Law of the Sea, the *Vega* was allowed to sail right to the edge of the twelve-mile territorial limit around Moruroa.

Cat and mouse

The crew did not have to wait long to find out that they were not welcome.

They had seen no sign of human life at sea for many days but, as dawn broke the next day, a plane swooped so low over the ship it caused the crew to duck instinctively. Undeterred, the yacht continued on to the bomb test site and hove to for the night just outside the twelve-mile limit.

The next day, through the mist, they saw the lights of a large French warship. From then on, whenever the *Vega* moved it was shadowed by a warship. The game of cat and mouse went on for many days.

The "Vega", pictured here, was one of the first in Greenpeace's ever-growing fleet. Often donated or bought cheaply, the organization's boats are reconditioned and maintained by volunteers.

Despite almost continuous rough weather that meant the crew had to be tied into their bunks to sleep and were soaked in sea water all the time, the *Vega* stayed close to the bomb site.

Although McTaggart had no way of knowing it, the *Vega* was being successful in delaying the tests. The French were fearful of the international reaction if they blew up a bomb and killed the crew.

But the French navy was frustrated and began running its warships perilously close to the yacht to try to frighten the crew. This was in spite of the international rules of the sea which say that steamships must give way to sail. They even raised a balloon above the coral reef to signal to McTaggart that they were about to let off the bomb and kill them. The *Vega* refused to leave.

Rammed and disabled

Frustration finally turned to anger. Orders were sent from France that the bomb tests were to go ahead. A new mood of determination overtook the French warship commanders. Even though the yacht was wooden, and like a matchbox compared with the steel French warships, they pressed McTaggart and his crew closer and closer to try and prevent them sailing back to Moruroa. Then the inevitable happened – a French minesweeper in heavy seas miscalculated and sliced into the starboard side of the *Vega*.

Although the *Vega* did not sink, it was so badly damaged that it could not survive for long in such rough waters and was not able to sail back to New Zealand without repairs. Despite their irritation with Greenpeace, some of the French sailors were appalled at what they had done. McTaggart was forced to submit to being towed into the nuclear test site where the French navy repaired the yacht – on condition that the *Vega* ended its protest. Exhausted and with few supplies remaining, the crew had no alternative but to agree.

The French bomb test went ahead as soon as the *Vega* was on its way home. The French appeared to have won that round, but their reaction had made McTaggart a determined and implacable opponent.

> *"...as McTaggart and his small crew reached the site for the bomb test, the French navy charged them with minesweepers and a 200-metre cruiser and buzzed them with helicopters and aircraft for eight days."*
>
> Fred Pearce,
> from "Green Warriors".

Breaking new ground

McTaggart began a long battle for compensation from the French for what he regarded as an act of piracy – ramming his vessel outside the twelve-mile limit. Despite promises of the Canadian government backing his case, politicians and civil servants were slow to act and the case dragged on for months. McTaggart eventually tired of this. When he heard that the French were going ahead with another season of weapon tests at Moruroa, he made up his mind to return.

The Greenpeace Foundation, together with David McTaggart's friends in New Zealand, raised enough money to repair the *Vega*. This time, McTaggart decided on a crew of four, two of whom would be women. They were Nigel Ingram from the first trip, Ann-Marie Horne and Mary Lornie, the girlfriends of the two men. It was the first time women had gone on such a protest.

Thereafter, mixed crews became normal for Greenpeace. Women have always been prominent in the environmental movement and McTaggart believed,

wrongly as it turned out, that their presence on this voyage would make the French more civilized in their approach. Similarly, a policy of mixed nationalities has been adopted. This has a dual purpose. The first is to reinforce the global nature of environmental problems and show that they are of concern to many races. The second is to gain more publicity for Greenpeace campaigns by grabbing the interest of journalists and governments in the fate of their fellow citizens on the ships.

Boarding party

The voyage to Moruroa was again long and hard and, as before, the French were waiting for the *Vega*. This time, they had decided that they were not going to let a tiny yacht bobbing about just outside the territorial limit delay the bomb tests. Using armed marines, the French chased and boarded the *Vega* and beat the two male crew members severely, even though they offered no resistance. Anne-Marie photographed the beating administered to McTaggart, whose eye was so badly damaged he required months of hospital treatment. The yacht was arrested and the crew deported.

Despite attempts by the French to deny what had happened and to confiscate cameras and film, the women crew managed to smuggle out pictures of the beating. These made worldwide coverage and showed the French authorities, who had said that their men were unarmed and had used no violence, to be liars.

This was not enough for McTaggart. Realizing that the Canadian government was not going to help because it was involved in selling uranium to the French for their nuclear weapons, he went directly to the courts. It was three years before McTaggart finally won compensation from the French navy.

Opposite top: David McTaggart lies injured in a hospital bed after he and another crew member, Nigel Ingram (opposite below), are beaten and bundled off the "Vega" by French military officers.

Save the whales

While McTaggart was taking on the French in the Pacific, Greenpeace was branching out elsewhere and membership was growing.

One of the members on the first nuclear protest, Robert Hunter, and a biologist, named Paul Spong, began campaigning against the continuing slaughter of whales. These huge creatures, the largest in the world and sometimes ten times bigger than an elephant, had been hunted for many centuries. But since 1900, so many had been killed that some species had been almost wiped out.

Instead of killing a few a year, hundreds of thousands of whales had been hunted by fleets of harpoon boats and processed while still at sea in factory ships. At one time the fat, or blubber, was boiled down to make oil. Originally, this was used for heating and lighting but, by the 1970s, there were many commercially-made substitutes available.

After World War II, whales had provided a source of cheap meat for the poorer people in Japan. Now Japan was much richer and, as the whales got rarer, the meat was becoming a luxury. So Robert Hunter and Paul Spong started to plan their campaign against the continued whaling by Japan and the then Soviet Union.

The two campaigners wanted to confront the whaling fleets on the high seas. They decided to use fast-moving inflatables, just as the French had used against David McTaggart in the Pacific. Once they had found the

Below: An 1825 painting of whalers in action. In those days, a few whales were harpooned and killed by hand each year. A century later, using an explosive harpoon, forty thousand whales were killed each season.

A breaching humpback whale looks magnificent as the water drains from its body. The population of these whales, once hundreds of thousands, is now feared to be down to two thousand in the southern hemisphere – due to over hunting.

"A whaling ship, an explosive harpoon, a fleeing whale and between them a tiny, manned inflatable with the word 'Greenpeace' emblazoned on its side - it says it all."

*Nick Gallie,
a Greenpeace member.*

whaling fleet, they would lower these fast boats into the water and race off to place themselves between the whales and the whalers. The harpooner, then, would not be able to get a clear shot at the whales.

Slaughter

In September 1974, the two men explained their ideas to a large group of volunteers. The following year the first proper Greenpeace office opened in Vancouver in Canada. The original boats, the *Phyllis Cormack* and the *Vega* (*Greenpeace* and *Greenpeace III*) were brought back into service.

The first task was to locate the whaling fleets. Posing as a whale researcher, Paul Spong went to Europe and obtained charts showing where Soviet and Japanese whaling fleets had hunted in previous years. Because of the limited range of the Greenpeace boats, Spong calculated that the protesters' best chance was to intercept the Soviet fleet when it passed within sixty miles of the California coast in June.

A recently-killed whale is cut up. Products from these huge animals included meat, oil for machinery and even cosmetics. Despite the fact that some of these products can now be made using synthetic materials, Norway, Iceland and Japan, traditional whaling nations, continually push to whale commercially.

An estimated twenty-three-thousand people were there to see the *Vega* and *Phyllis Cormack* sail. After more than a month at sea, a radio signal from the Soviet factory ship, the *Dalniy Vostok,* was intercepted. This was the ship where the freshly-killed whales were butchered, cut into steaks, and their blubber boiled down into oil. Within days, the Soviet fleet was in sight. The whalers had attached a marker beacon to a whale that they had just killed so they could come back for it. The sea around it was red with blood from the still-bleeding corpse.

The Greenpeace crew could see that the whale, while huge, was still not fully grown. The Soviet hunters had been caught breaking their own rules: killing juvenile whales.

Two inflatables were placed in the water to buzz the factory ship. The protesters filmed the dead whales being hauled up the slipway into the processing area. Blood gushed into the sea. The protesters then switched tactics and chased a harpoon boat, the *Vlastny*. Spouts from a family of whales could be seen in the

distance as the *Vlastny* closed in for the kill. In one of the inflatables, Robert Hunter and George Korotva raced to put themselves between the harpoon guns and the whale. At the same time, other Greenpeace members filmed from the other inflatable, as the Soviets fired their harpoon over the heads of the Greenpeace crew and it plunged into a whale a few yards away. The grenade in the harpoon exploded in the creature's back. The whale bled to death as the Soviets hauled it alongside.

This close encounter had been captured on film and was soon to be famous.

Faced with horror, as blood gushes from the portholes of a whaling ship, Greenpeace demand a stop to the killing. "Save the Whale" has been one of Greenpeace's most high-profile campaigns, attracting much public support and media attention.

Greenpeace grows

Although the first whale had died, the Greenpeace crew continued to harry the Soviet fleet and saved at least another eight whales from the exploding harpoons.

As the Soviets sailed away, the *Phyllis Cormack* motored back to San Francisco. The journalists on board had been radioing their reports back to newspapers and wire services all over North America. This meant that more journalists were waiting to greet them, as well as a huge crowd of supporters and well-wishers. The mission had been an unqualified success.

Even more than the nuclear issue, the courage of Greenpeace members facing death to make a point about protecting the environment had captured public imagination and Greenpeace groups grew up in many places. By 1976, there were said to be ten thousand supporters, although most of the groups were run from the homes of individual enthusiasts, rather than offices.

That year, Greenpeace raised enough money to finance a second trip against the Soviet whalers and hired a bigger, faster boat with room for a crew of thirty-six. Remembering the legend of the Cree Indian woman, Eyes of Fire, the volunteers painted a rainbow on the bow of the new ship. This time the protesters were able to sail further and take on the whaling fleet for longer. On their return, the campaigners claimed they had saved a hundred whales.

A nine-ton minke whale is hauled up the slipway of the "Nisshin Maru". The Japanese factory ship processed 330 dead whales in 1992, despite Greenpeace attempts to stop the hunt. The Japanese call it "scientific whaling" to assess the size and age of the stocks, but the valuable meat is sold by Japanese restaurants as a luxury dish.

Disappearing whales

Although the protest missions were attracting more members and plenty of publicity, Greenpeace realized this alone would not solve any problems. In the case of whaling, all decisions about the industry were taken by the International Whaling Commission. This organization had been established in 1946 by the whaling nations to regulate the industry because of widespread fears that the whales would be wiped out altogether if there weren't controls on indiscriminate hunting. The idea was to "properly conserve the whale stocks" and "make possible the orderly development of the whaling industry".

Scientists were employed to decide how many

whales could be killed each season without reducing the stock so much that eventually whales would become extinct. Each year, the scientists recommended lower and lower catches. Each year, the whaling nations, like the Soviet Union and Norway, ignored them and killed more, so the number of whales available to be hunted for the following year was steadily being reduced. For example in 1900, there were estimated to be 250,000 of the world's largest whale, the blue whale, which can reach a weight of 150 tons. By 1972, it was calculated this number had been reduced to six thousand, but the slaughter continued. A count at the end of the 1980s put the world population as low as four hundred. No one knows whether the species can now survive.

The killing continues

Over the years, as each of the largest whale species nearly disappeared, the hunters switched to the smaller types, that had previously been considered too small to bother with. Greenpeace, and a number of other conservation groups, decided that the only way to save the whales was to influence the decisions taken by the

"For more than sixty years, the Southern Ocean was the world's major whaling ground. The whaling industry was so intensive that the blue whale population now stands at less than one per cent of its original level."

John May,
from "The Greenpeace
Book of Antarctica".

Greenpeace stages a non-violent protest to draw attention to the plight of the whales. The blue whale behind the railings reminds us that the population of this species is dangerously low.

International Whaling Commission. Attempts were made to impose a ten-year ban on commercial whaling while stocks were re-counted and assessed.

It was 1985 before a ban finally came into effect although some nations, including Japan, continue to kill whales. Instead of calling it commercial whaling, Japan describes the killing as scientific. They say that by killing whales they can find out the age, sex and breeding success of the creatures. Greenpeace believe this is just an excuse for keeping the whaling industry alive, pointing out that the meat is still sold for profit in Japanese restaurants.

In 1986 Greenpeace converted a Dutch fishing vessel into a campaign boat, called *Moby Dick,* to harrass the Norwegian whalers. A crew of eleven, from six countries, contrived to get themselves arrested twice and fined for boarding and occupying the Norwegian harpoon boats.

By the end of the season the Norwegian government promised it would cease commercial whaling.

Dolphins at risk

Once Greenpeace had branched out from the single issue of attempting to stop nuclear testing to saving whales, a whole series of different environmental campaigns began.

As early as 1978, the plight of dolphins being killed in their hundreds by Japanese fishermen had shocked the organization's members. Many species of these beautiful creatures are killed for their meat and are disappearing from the seas. Greenpeace want the hunting of rare dolphins banned and are trying to get the International Whaling Commission to protect them in the same way as their larger cousins, the whales.

Another threat is the accidental killing of dolphins in long, nylon nets called drift-nets. These are some-times many miles long and are used in the Pacific to catch tuna fish.

In 1990, Greenpeace strengthened its protests against the use of these nets, after finding many dol-phins trapped in them. The dolphins could not get to the surface to breathe and had drowned. The use of very long nets has now been banned by the United Nations,

out dolphins still get caught and drown. Attempts are being made to design new nets to allow dolphins, whales, sunfish and other species, not wanted by fishermen, to escape before they are accidently killed.

Clubbed to death

Another campaign was to save baby seals, which were being wiped out in their thousands each March.

At first, harp seals are pure white to blend in with the Arctic ice on which they are born, changing after two weeks as they follow their darker-furred mothers into the water. Each spring, hundreds of Canadian and Norwegian sealers hurried to the ice to club the creatures to death and skin them. The skins were made into fur coats in Europe and America. The barbaric practice of clubbing desirable, white baby seals to death, to the cries of terror from the helpless mothers, was captured on film and shown on television. Many viewers all over the world were shocked. Greenpeace volunteers and the International Fund for Animal Welfare (IFAW) were

Dolphins (opposite top) are herded together by the Japanese, near Tokyo. Then, (opposite below) preventing their escape with nets, they are slaughtered. Some are eaten, while others are used for pig food and in fertilizer.

Below: A Greenpeace diver swims to the aid of a rare sunfish caught in a Japanese drift-net in the Tasman Sea, south of Australia. These nets entangle an estimated 120,000 dolphins, whales and seals every year. The United Nations now regulates the use of these nets to cut the indiscriminate killing.

Above: A trail of blood shows where a seal pup has been clubbed to death and dragged across the ice.

Opposite top: Killed in the first three weeks of life while their fur is still white, it takes dozens of harp seals, like this one, to make one fur coat.

Opposite below: A harmless green dye is sprayed on the helpless seal pup to make its coat worthless.

among a number of campaigners determined to stop this cruel killing.

The first idea Greenpeace came up with was to spray the pups with a harmless green dye, making the pelts useless and giving the pups time to be weaned and swim out to the safety of the sea. This tactic almost led to violence by the sealers against Greenpeace in Canadian Newfoundland. The Canadian government responded by making the spraying of pups with green dye a criminal offence.

Volunteers then wrapped their arms around the seals and used themselves as human shields to prevent the pups being clubbed. In temperatures of -20°C, the going was tough. Many individual pups were saved by the volunteers, but they could not stop the main slaughter.

New tactics

The battle between the sealers and animal welfare campaigners became an annual event. Each year, Greenpeace was growing in strength and was able to get people from many different places to help. Some got in touch with newspapers and television stations to draw their attention to the campaign and others went to the scene.

One of those who joined the annual battle, bringing with him a television crew, was David McTaggart. Despite the pressure, more and more laws were passed by the Canadian government to try to allow the seal hunt to continue. McTaggart and other campaigners began to realize that, having won public opinion, the real solution lay away from the killing fields.

Most of the seal pelts were imported into Europe to be made into fashion clothing. So campaigners concentrated on convincing European politicians that the trade in pelts should be banned. They lobbied governments and wrote to members of parliament demanding that the Canadian government be asked to stop the killing. In January 1983, pressure was mounting. Just before the annual hunt was due to begin, the biggest commercial trader, Norway, announced it would end the killing of all seal pups.

By the following year, the European Community had

banned the import of all seal goods and the seal hunt was severely restricted. In frustration, the hunters destroyed an IFAW helicopter, which had made an emergency landing. Also, a Greenpeace aircraft was seized by the authorities and the crew arrested.

"Rainbow Warrior"

As Greenpeace volunteers took on more and more campaigns, membership and the number of branches grew. David McTaggart set about organizing offices in various countries in Europe. He formed a link with Friends of the Earth in London and, in 1977, four people formed Greenpeace UK. In France, a young activist, Remi Parmentier, set up a French branch.

The following year, Greenpeace Netherlands was established, and the Dutch branch of the World Wildlife Fund agreed to provide a grant to finance a campaign against Icelandic whaling. A ship was bought with the money, an ex-fishing research vessel; it was in a sorry state, but was transformed by volunteers. The word

"Greenpeace" was painted on the side along with a dove of peace. Inspired by the early Indian legends it was called "Rainbow Warrior".

Elsewhere, however, the Greenpeace organization was falling apart. In North America, matters had become chaotic. Strong personalities, who were prepared to risk their lives to save whales or go to prison for their beliefs, also had strong views about how their organization should be run. They frequently clashed with each other and debts were run up as money required for campaigns outstripped fund-raising efforts.

In 1977, one of the pioneers, Robert Hunter, resigned as president, and Paul Watson, accused of arguing over tactics on whaling, was removed from the board of directors after a bitter dispute. The Vancouver office ran up serious debts and, as clashes continued, various breakaway groups were formed – all calling themselves Greenpeace.

Nuclear dumping

While much energy was being wasted on internal disputes in North America, the *Rainbow Warrior* was still engaging in action to protect the whales, this time against the Icelandic whalers.

In June 1978, the new ship headed south to take action against another whaling nation, Spain, but decided to divert to another cause on the way. For many years, the nuclear nations of Europe had been using the seas off the European coast as a dumping ground for their nuclear waste. On the charts, an area of sea was marked "dumping area" six hundred miles off the south-west coast of England. In America, putting this type of waste into the sea had been abandoned on environmental grounds back in 1972. The leader of the Greenpeace campaign, Peter Wilkinson, felt strongly that a protest should be made about the continuation of the practice in Europe.

The protest was spurred on by information that the next dump was to contain spent fuel rods from nuclear submarines – nuclear waste so dangerous that dumping it in the sea was outlawed by international treaties. The nuclear dump ship, the *Gem,* left the docks, chased by the *Rainbow Warrior* six hours behind.

Opposite: The "Rainbow Warrior" in full sail. It was bought by Greenpeace in February 1978, transformed by volunteers and put into action in less than three months: it became the flagship of the organization.

Below: Making their presence known, Greenpeace campaigners chain themselves to a ship dumping toxic industrial waste in the Mersey estuary off Liverpool, in the UK.

Volunteers go into action against a cargo vessel, to try to prevent the delivery of parts for the Sizewell B nuclear plant, in the UK.

"Greenpeace has forced Britain to change direction regarding its policy on toxic discharges to the marine environment and on its policy on dumping radioactive waste at sea."

From a Greenpeace campaign report, 1993.

When the Greenpeace ship finally reached the dumping zone, the rubber dinghies were lowered into the water. Volunteers raced up to the *Gem* and put themselves below the dumping platform to prevent the nuclear waste being thrown into the sea. Without regard for the volunteers' safety, the dumping continued and one of the barrels, weighing a ton, was dropped onto an inflatable. It just missed killing the crew, but destroyed the outboard motor and deflated one of the panels of the boat. The entire incident had been filmed from the bridge of the *Rainbow Warrior* and, when it was later shown on television, it damaged the reputation of the dumpers. On his return to Britain, Wilkinson began to take on the nuclear industry in earnest.

By 1985, he had the transport trade unions on his side, refusing to move barrels of waste to the docks for dumping. That year, the British government, the last nuclear dumper in Europe, abandoned the practice and began looking for sites on land.

By that time, Greenpeace had begun to campaign about many aspects of nuclear power. The reprocessing plant at Sellafield in north-west Britain, which poured plutonium and other dangerous waste into the sea, was accused of causing a type of cancer in the children of the area.

Greenpeace is still continuing to demand the plant be closed and for an end to the transportation of spent nuclear fuel and plutonium around the world.

"Greenpeace believes that transportation of dangerous waste makes accidents and spills more likely and that allowing international transport of waste does not encourage industry to use cleaner methods."

Michael Brown and John May, from "The Greenpeace Story".

Greenpeace International

Meanwhile in 1978, the *Rainbow Warrior* and its crew of volunteers were fast becoming celebrities. From taking on the nuclear dumpers in June, it went on to Spain to tackle the Spanish whaling fleet in August, narrowly escaping arrest by the Spanish navy. In October, the ship was off the Orkney Islands to the north of Scotland, defending seals which the local fishermen claimed were reducing fish stocks. The British government abandoned the plan to kill half the seals after receiving 16,500 letters of protest from Greenpeace supporters.

While the organization increased its membership and was becoming well known in Europe, the North American groups were getting further and further into difficulty. The Vancouver office was hugely in debt. San Francisco, on the other hand, was financially successful, but was accused by the Vancouver office of cashing in on the Greenpeace name. Greenpeace Vancouver finally decided to sue San Francisco for violation of their trademark. San Francisco retaliated by suing Vancouver for slander. The court case threatened to destroy the organization.

McTaggart, who had been so successful in creating the European organization, flew in to be a peacemaker. Under his guidance, the United States and Toronto officers met the Vancouver members to try to make a deal. In the end Greenpeace Europe agreed to pay off Vancouver's debts. In return, all the groups decided to join together under one co-ordinated organization: Greenpeace International. David McTaggart, the architect of the agreement, was made chief executive officer and chairman.

In dramatic style, Greenpeace protesters use harmless materials to draw attention to the dangers of nuclear waste. Hundreds of thousands of barrels are stored in Europe, despite there being no solution to disposing of them safely.

Opposite top: A scandal develops as Greenpeace uncover highly-toxic mercury waste in a landfill pit in Spain. The mercury mined in Spain is used worldwide for the manufacture of such things as batteries and chlorine. Mercury waste is difficult and expensive to dispose of properly, so it was being secretly exported back to Spain to be dumped.

Opposite below: To draw attention to the dangerous chemicals being pumped into Europe's rivers, Greenpeace adopted a policy of blocking waste pipes. Here in June 1992, volunteers plug the Rhône Poulenc outflow into the River Seine, near Rouen in northern France.

Dictatorship or democracy?

Under McTaggart's leadership the organization worked far better, although many felt it was more of a dictatorship than a democracy. The problems of running an organization like Greenpeace often demanded secrecy. When a Greenpeace ship was going on a mission of direct action, only the captain and the campaigner on board knew exactly what was going to happen. The crew and many of those in the offices were not told for fear of an information leak which would prepare the authorities or risk court injunctions to prevent actions starting.

Not everyone could crew the ships and climb chimneys, only the most highly-skilled of the hundreds of volunteers were selected. The ordinary supporters, confined to writing letters, raising money by selling T-shirts or going on sponsored walks and cycle rides, sometimes felt cut off from the decision-making and the action.

The International Board was elected with two representatives from the continents of Europe, North America and Australasia. With McTaggart firmly in charge as chairman, the Board decided on its priorities each year. Major campaigns were planned on a worldwide basis. When television news in a dozen

Right: David McTaggart, who became involved with Greenpeace when he first sailed his yacht, "Vega", into the French nuclear test zone, in 1972. Seven years later, McTaggart was appointed chairman of the International Board of Greenpeace.

countries carried pictures of Greenpeace in action, there was no doubt of the success of McTaggart's methods.

By early 1980, there were twenty-five-thousand paying supporters. There were groups in Canada, Australia, France, the Netherlands, New Zealand, the United Kingdom and the United States, which alone had nine regional offices. In the Netherlands, new members were being signed on at the rate of 1,100 a month. McTaggart kept out of the public gaze, encouraging his campaigners to appear on radio and television, while he ran the organization from behind the scenes.

The first international office was in England which was then moved to Amsterdam in the Netherlands where it remains. Each national organization gives a quarter of its income to Greenpeace International to run the ships and organize campaigns around the world.

Toxic dumping

Environmental issues, in which Greenpeace became involved, began to widen further. One successful early campaign had been against the excessive use of pesticides that had been wiping out wildlife in British Columbian forests. In Europe, particularly in the Netherlands and Germany, the use of toxic chemicals and their disposal in rivers and the sea became one of the major causes for concern.

The first success in Europe was against the giant chemical company, Bayer. In 1980, the *Rainbow Warrior*, helped by five other vessels, blockaded dump vessels in Rotterdam. They were intended to put ten thousand tonnes of acid waste in the North Sea. By the time the blockade was called off, the dumping issue was front-page news and had damaged Bayer's reputation. That dump went ahead but, two years later, under increasing pressure, the company finally abandoned the practice.

Many cases of pollution were revealed by a Greenpeace vessel, the *Beluga*. Originally a river fire-fighting vessel, it had been transformed by volunteers and named after a species of small white whale. It was equipped with a laboratory, a special computer and scientific equipment capable of identifying chemical

Hanging in protest, Greenpeace activists abseil from the Leverkusen Bridge over the River Rhine, in Germany, 1986. This was to draw attention to the huge amount of toxic waste that flows from the Rhine into the North Sea each year.

waste. The *Beluga* toured the inland waters of Europe monitoring pollution in the rivers Rhine, Elbe, Schelde, Seine, Weser, Meuse, Thames, Humber, Severn, Tyne, Tees and Mersey. The coastal waters of Denmark, Sweden, the Netherlands and the United Kingdom were also sampled. Many of the results showed high levels of pollution.

A change of emphasis

As Greenpeace expanded, ideas and demands for new campaigns also grew. The whereabouts and activities of the increasing fleet of ships was logged on huge maps of the world. The International Board allocated money for the campaigns and the latest radio and computer technology was used for ships, offices and campaigners to talk to each other.

Below left: Flounders, showing terrible lesions on their skin. Pollution makes the fish vulnerable to bacterial and viral infections.

Below: A French dump ship is caught in action, getting rid of its cargo of phosphogypsum, used in fertilizers, which adds unwanted nutrients into the sea.

After the collapse of communism, Greenpeace was able to open an office in Kiev, in the Ukraine. Here, scientists take soil and plant samples to check on radiation levels, to see if locally-grown food is safe to eat.

In the early days, all the emphasis had been on direct action but, as support grew and issues became more complex, Greenpeace began to do more and more scientific research. In between campaigns, ships were used as mobile laboratories to test the environment and university research departments analyzed the results.

In the late 1970s and early 1980s, the priorities were slightly different. As funds became available, volunteers scoured the docks for second-hand trawlers and other tough vessels to adapt for Greenpeace use. The steady flow of volunteers ensured that expert help was given at virtually no cost to the organization. By the early 1990s, Greenpeace had full-time scientists of international reputation working for it.

Evacuating an island

As part of the International Board's wish to be capable of reaching any part of the globe to raise environmental issues, Greenpeace decided to fit the *Rainbow Warrior* with sails. It also suited the organization's image to use wind power rather than burn fuel. A member of the Greenpeace International Board, Steve Sawyer, was in charge of a new expedition to sail the Pacific. The crew were to set off on a voyage to visit the far-flung islands of Hawaii, the Marshalls, Kiribati, Vanuatu and New Zealand before the final leg of the journey to take on the old enemy, the French nuclear testers at Moruroa.

The *Warrior* left America on March 15, 1985. Greenpeace was to attempt its most ambitious mission yet in the Marshall Islands. In the far north of the island group, on what appeared to be a paradise coral island, Rongalap, lived a troubled and sick people. Between 1946 and 1958 that area of the Pacific had been used for atmospheric nuclear tests. The islanders had more than once been in the path of radioactive fallout and, although evacuated before, they had been returned to the islands and reassured they were safe.

Fallout makes people feel sick and burns the skin during the first few days. They appear to get better but then other ailments develop. Many of the islanders became ill. They had to take pills daily to keep them well but some, including young children, developed

Sea water is regularly sampled in Antarctica to see if pollutants are reaching the area from other parts of the globe. The minute sea creatures, which live close to the surface of the sea, are checked to see if they are affected by increased ultraviolet light, caused by the hole in the ozone layer.

cancer and died. Adults prematurely aged, a sure sign of being exposed to excessive radiation. They were warned not to eat local vegetables, fruit and coconuts because these contained plutonium. The plutonium had fallen in the cloud of radioactive dust from the nuclear tests and was now in all the plants and fish. Canned food was delivered to the people twice a year by the Americans, but they were refused any other help. Convinced that they had been abandoned in a dangerous area as some sort of experiment, the people appealed to Greenpeace for help. In May 1985, the *Rainbow Warrior* arrived at Rongalap.

The plan was to move the entire population, all their possessions and most of their makeshift homes to another safer island ten hours' sailing away. It took four exhausting trips over two weeks to establish the three hundred islanders in their new home. All that was left standing of their original village was the pure white church and the graveyard where many young children had been laid to a premature rest.

"Many vomited and felt weak. Later, the hair of men, women and children began to fall out. A lot of people had burns on their skin. The Americans came and told us not to drink the water. They explained we were in great danger."

John Anjain, an islander from Rongelap.

Shortly after, on July 10, 1985, an event occurred that was to shock the world and change the course of Greenpeace's history.

The first part of the *Rainbow Warrior's* voyage across the Pacific had been an unqualified success. The ship, with its newly-fitted sails, had attracted large crowds wherever it had gone. It finally arrived in New Zealand where, as Greenpeace's flagship, its arrival was treated as an important event. Thirty small craft and

Overshadowed, but not intimidated, Greenpeace activists pitch their tiny inflatables against the US nuclear aircraft carrier, "Eisenhower", in a protest against nuclear dumping at sea.

hundreds of people turned out to greet the *Rainbow Warrior* in Auckland.

It was time for the crew to make final preparations for the next and most-testing part of the voyage: another confrontation with the French navy at Moruroa to stop the testing of a new and more terrible nuclear device, the neutron bomb. This time the protest would be even bigger than before – to reflect the increased membership and strength of the organization. The *Rainbow*

"I saw Greenpeace as an icon, a symbol from which we might affect the attitudes of millions of people towards their environment."

Robert Hunter, a former Canadian journalist and Greenpeace activist.

Warrior was to act as a mother ship carrying supplies and small boats. It would be accompanied by the *Vega*, which had made the first pioneer protest voyage to Moruroa as *Greenpeace III*, thirteen years before. Another yacht, the *Fri*, would arrive at Moruroa from the Caribbean. From Tahiti, the French colony in the middle of the Pacific, some Polynesian people, anxious to gain their independence from France, were planning to join the Greenpeace protest.

Secret agent

In March 1985, when the French Ministry of Defence had learned that Greenpeace was going to make another voyage to Moruroa, plans were made to stop them. A secret agent, Christine Cabon, using a false name and posing as an ecologist, was sent to New Zealand to infiltrate the Greenpeace Auckland office. Her job was to find out about their operations and inform her bosses back in Paris. Since Greenpeace is happy to accept help from volunteers, the spy found it easy to gain the trust of the people in New Zealand and was even given somewhere free to stay.

Other agents, specially trained as underwater divers and saboteurs, were picked to crew a yacht called the *Ouvea*. While the *Rainbow Warrior* was still out in the Pacific at the end of June, they sailed into a lonely bay in North Island, New Zealand, posing as tourists. They had secretly brought with them explosives, diving gear and a fast inflatable dinghy. At Auckland airport another team of agents arrived. They were posing as a Swiss honeymoon couple, Alain and Sophie Turenge, but, in reality, they were French spies, Major Alain Mafart and Captain Dominique Prieur. The following day, Colonel Louis-Pierre Dillais also arrived by air – he would be in charge of the coming operation.

Bombed

The *Rainbow Warrior* did not arrive until July 7, several days after the French agents had gathered and made their plans. After a welcoming party, the crew settled down to cleaning the ship and renewing the painted rainbow and dove of peace on the prow. On the evening of July 10, there was a birthday party on board. The leader of that year's voyage across the Pacific, Steve Sawyer, was twenty-nine. A big birthday cake had been made by the ship's cook and everyone on board was given a piece.

Despite the celebrations, Steve Sawyer had to leave the party early. There were important plans to make and he had to meet Greenpeace visitors. There was nothing to make the crew believe they were in any danger. Some of them had already gone to their bunks below the water line and were asleep. Others were still talking over a beer in the ship's mess room.

Suddenly, at 11:38 p.m. a bomb went off. Cushioned by the water, it sounded like a dull thud outside, but on board the *Rainbow Warrior* it was powerful enough to lift people out of their seats.

The explosion tore a three-foot-wide hole in the hull of the ship and thousands of gallons of water poured into the engine room.

Abandon ship!

It was clear the ship was sinking. There was confusion as members of the crew searched for friends. Captain Peter Willcox ordered everyone to abandon ship and

Bombed by the French secret service, the "Rainbow Warrior" lies crippled at her moorings in the port of Auckland, New Zealand, July 1985. The French had learned that the ship was preparing to sail for Moruroa to try and disrupt their continuing nuclear tests.

39

people began scrambling for the quayside. The ship's doctor went to check the cabins below and pulled the cook, Margaret Mills, to safety. She had been asleep when the bomb went off. The expedition photographer, Fernando Pereira, went below to retrieve his most precious possessions, his cameras. They were in his cabin and would be ruined if they were swamped by the sea. He was not to know that the French frogmen had planted a second bomb underwater – outside the cabin wall next to where the crew slept. It was timed to go off two minutes after the first. As Fernando groped in the dark for his cameras, the bomb exploded next to him, knocking him out. He drowned as the water poured in over him.

Out on the deck, the last of the crew leapt to safety as the ship keeled over and lay on its side. The Greenpeace flagship, on which they had just sailed thousands of miles across the Pacific, had been destroyed. Their fellow crew member and friend, Fernando Pereira, was dead, the first Greenpeace volunteer to die in the cause. They were stunned with shock and sadness.

The Greenpeace photographer, Fernando Pereira, was killed when the French blew up the "Rainbow Warrior". He was the first volunteer to die. With the French denying responsibility for the blast for months, justice for Pereira's death was never fully achieved.

Guilty

Acts of terrorism were unknown in New Zealand before the bombing of the *Rainbow Warrior,* but the police acted quickly. At first, both Greenpeace and the police were unwilling to believe bombs could have been planted and people murdered by agents of the French government. But as the investigation progressed, it was clear it was so. In the beginning the French denied it and even an official government investigation in Paris declared that no senior officials or politicians were involved.

But, on September 17, more than two months after the bombing, the French newspaper, *Le Monde,* declared that Admiral Lacoste and his boss, the minister of defence, Charles Hernu, were both aware of the sabotage operation and had probably ordered it. Two days later, Admiral Lacoste was dismissed from his job and the defence minister resigned.

On the evening of Sunday, September 22, the prime minister of France went on television and admitted that the secret agents had sunk the boat on government orders. Six of the eight agents, known to have taken part in the sabotage and murder operation, escaped and were protected by the French government from prosecution. Only two, Mafart and Prieur, who had posed as the honeymoon couple, were caught. There was no proof that they had actually planted the explosives, so they pleaded guilty to manslaughter and wilful damage. They were each sentenced to ten years in prison.

On July 8, 1986, they were released from prison in New Zealand and confined to the French military atoll of Hao for three years. It was part of a deal in which the French government paid New Zealand seven million dollars in compensation for the terrorist attack on the *Rainbow Warrior*. At the same time, the French government made a formal apology to New Zealand. The French also paid undisclosed damages to Fernando Pereira's widow and two children.

"You can't sink a Rainbow"

Despite the hopes of Greenpeace members worldwide, the *Rainbow Warrior* had been so badly damaged it could not be refloated and repaired. Instead, all the machinery was taken out and the hull adapted so it could be used as an underwater haven for fish to breed. It was towed out to sea and, at a special ceremony, found a final resting place where it could help marine conservation.

Rather than discourage Greenpeace members, the sabotage and sinking of the *Rainbow Warrior* made them more determined. Under the slogan "You can't sink a Rainbow", Greenpeace immediately began to collect money for a new ship. Worldwide sympathy and shock at what had happened translated into hundreds of thousands of new members in many countries. Nor was the protest to Moruroa abandoned.

Another ship, which had been kitted out for a new campaign in the Antarctic, was immediately diverted to the Pacific. The idea was that it should act as a mother ship off Moruroa to replace the *Rainbow Warrior*.

Money and supplies were given by trade unions and people from all walks of life in New Zealand to help the protest. The *Vega* sailed from New Zealand with the

"Far from being deterred or defeated, Greenpeace was, in the next few years, to spread its name, influence and activities across a wider landscape."
Michael Brown and John May, from "The Greenpeace Story".

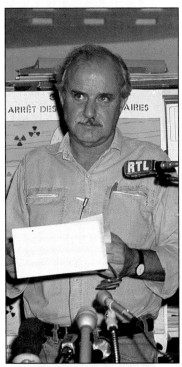

Chairman and chief executive of Greenpeace, David McTaggart, in solemn mood at a press conference demanding that those responsible for the terrorist attack of the "Rainbow Warrior" be brought to justice.

skipper of the *Rainbow Warrior* and one of the crew on board. Three more sailing vessels, the *Alliance*, the *Vanangian* and the *Breeze*, went too.

Warships wait for Greenpeace

The French were now faced with a bigger protest fleet than the one they had originally tried to stop. But they had three warships waiting at Moruroa. Another one shadowed the *Greenpeace* across the Pacific. They all had commandos as extra crew ready to board the Greenpeace vessels and arrest them. Despite the largest peace flotilla ever assembled, the French were determined to go ahead with their bomb tests.

On October 17, the Greenpeace mother ship was forced to abandon its vigil outside the territorial waters because one of its electricity generators broke down. The yachts stayed on, watched by the French warships. The underground test was set for the following week, whether the yachts remained on station or not.

In a final bid to stop the test, the *Vega* sailed straight for the bomb test site. After a chase, eight French commandos boarded the vessel and arrested the three crew. The test went ahead despite world condemnation.

Greenpeace members vowed that they would be back again.

"The near pristine and fragile nature of Antarctica's environment demands special treatment. Not only does it contain unique life forms but, as we have seen, its relatively untouched nature provides us with invaluable baseline information for understanding complex and diverse planetary systems."

John May,
from "The Greenpeace Book of Antarctica".

Adventures in the ice

Immediately after the Moruroa protest, Greenpeace began a campaign to turn Antarctica into a World Park.

For the volunteers, it meant a series of adventures in the most dangerous and least-explored part of the world.

Antarctica is a series of mountain ranges covered in a layer of ice. The ice is so thick and heavy that it literally presses the mountains back down into the earth's crust. The total land area is bigger than the United States or the whole of Europe. The two-mile-thick ice sheet sitting on top contains about 90% of the world's freshwater. The continent is so cold and remote that it was the last place on earth to be discovered by humankind. It has never been colonized because it is impossible to survive there without special equipment.

Above: An iceberg floats on the quiet waters of McMurdo Sound, in Antarctica. Beneath the surface lie hundreds of tons of rubbish dumped by the Americans. Under pressure from Greenpeace, some of it has been fished out and returned to the United States.

Left: The untouched beauty of Antarctica taken from the deck of the Greenpeace ship, the "Gondwana", is captured here by a crew member.

Above: After the removal of the Greenpeace World Park Base on the shore of the Ross Sea, scientists take samples to check for any atmospheric pollution trapped in the snow.

Right: Greenpeace scientists at the Scott Base in Antarctica monitor the hole in the ozone layer. They form part of an international team of observers that is scattered over the frozen continent.

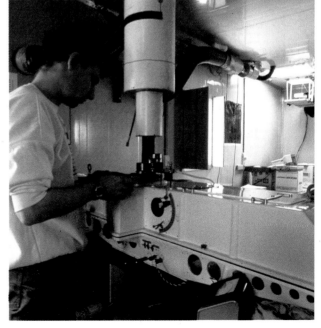

It might seem odd that Greenpeace should bother with such a place since it is the least-polluted land on earth. But that is exactly why the organization decided it was so important.

Scientists who work there are using the unpolluted atmosphere as a clean window through which they can study the stars, check on the protective ozone layer and monitor how the climate is changing. They have discovered it is possible to take a long section through the ice going back 150,000 years. Every year, a tiny amount of fresh snow that falls is gradually compressed into ice as the centuries pass. In each tiny annual layer, air is trapped. When liberated from the ice in a laboratory, the scientists are able to tell what gases were in the atmosphere all those centuries ago and relate it to the climate then.

Scientists are still trying to find out what makes the atmosphere heat up and cool down. They also want to study the ice to see if it is melting. The ice cap in Antarctica has been building up for sixteen million years, allowing the world's sea levels to fall. If the world is heating up and the ice cap melts, big areas of the world will flood again, including parts of countries like Bangladesh and Holland. Some low-lying Pacific island nations will disappear altogether.

A special place

Greenpeace believed that the wildlife of Antarctica – the whales, the penguins and the other special plants and animals that have adapted to the extreme cold – should be left in peace. The politicians did not agree.

Politicians knew that, many millions of years ago, Antarctica was joined to South America, Australia, Africa and India. In all these continents there were gold, oil, diamonds and other valuable minerals, like platinum, that could make countries rich. Governments began to develop ideas for digging up parts of Antarctica. Oil wells could be sunk around the rim of the continent, and precious metals extracted from the rocks that stick out from under the edge of the ice sheet.

Greenpeace realized that the hunt for minerals could destroy this unique place, but the politicians were not prepared to listen to protests. Nations decided to sign a

The second woman to over-winter in the Antarctic for Greenpeace, Dr. Sabine Schmidt, takes notes of measurements of water conditions below the sea ice in McMurdo Sound. This was part of a four-year scientific study at the World Park Base.

45

"They [the Treaty states who 'manage' Antarctica] are at this moment busily negotiating the mineral exploitation of Antarctica – behind closed doors, of course. We must put a stop to this before we lose the last paradise on Earth."

John May,
from "The Greenpeace
Book of Antarctica".

Below: Even on the remote island of South Georgia, Greenpeace members find a gentoo penguin with oil coated on its breast – illustrating the spread of industrial pollution.

new treaty, which was proposing to carve up the continent, so prospecting for minerals could begin. Greenpeace felt the only way to get its voice heard was to get the public on its side.

Save Antarctica

To do this Greenpeace sent a ship to the Antarctic taking journalists and visiting bases of the treaty nations. In this way, attention could be drawn to what the politicians were proposing to do. At the same time, Greenpeace could keep an eye on any secret activities that were damaging the environment. Volunteers

helped to kit out a coastguard cutter, which had been donated to Greenpeace, and it temporarily became the flagship of the organization after the *Rainbow Warrior* was sunk.

Greenpeace also decided to set up their own scientific base in Antarctica. This was partly to show how a model base could be run. All waste, including sewage, was to be recycled and taken home each year. Electricity would mostly be generated by wind power, and when the base was finally dismantled, Greenpeace believed that it would be able to take everything back home with it, without leaving a mark on the Antarctic landscape.

Rockhopper penguins stretch as far as the eye can see. They congregate in vast colonies to breed. The French moved many penguins, such as these, into pens in order to demolish their nesting areas, to make way for an intended airstrip at Dumont d'Urville, in Antarctica.

"If we can't leave this place [Antarctica] as it is – when there is no immediate need for its hidden mineral wealth, when there is sufficient time to find renewable alternatives, and when there is a degree of international cooperation in Antarctic science – how can we possibly hope to reverse the destructive tide in other areas of the world?"

Kelly Rigg,
*international coordinator for the
Greenpeace Antarctic campaign.*

As the ship set off on its first expedition, every Greenpeace office in the world began to campaign to save Antarctica. From the beginning everyone knew it would be a difficult task, many critics, even supporters, said it was impossible. Just getting people interested in the Antarctic was difficult. For a start, many people do not know whether Antarctica is at the North or South Pole and only have a remote idea of what Antarctica is like. For example, in winter it is dark for three months and in summer the sun does not set for a similar period. It was going to be hard to explain why such a strange inhospitable place should be saved.

Icebergs

The sailing conditions for the crew were worse than anyone could have imagined. The Southern Ocean is the roughest in the world, and huge waves and the wind battered the ship as it struggled south.

Once into colder areas, there was the hazard of icebergs, some hardly visible below the waves, others

more than a mile across and high like cliffs. Icebergs are pieces of freshwater ice that have broken off the main ice cap and drift around for years on the currents, getting gradually smaller and smaller as the months pass. Because the ice is so old and compressed, it is harder than steel and the crew had to keep twenty-four-hour iceberg watch. To hit one iceberg could have holed the ship and, even if the vessel had not sunk, an accident would have meant abandoning the voyage.

As the ship got further south the crew met another hazard – sea ice. This is frozen sea water which forms every winter and then breaks up and drifts around in the summer. It's often called pack ice because it drifts together and packs around ships and other objects. On this first expedition, ice conditions around the continent were the worst for thirty years. The Greenpeace ship became trapped in the ice in the Ross Sea and the crew feared they might be squashed. Another ship, which was slightly closer to the continent, was even more entangled in the pack ice. It was crushed like an eggshell as two great pieces of sea ice drifted together.

Brought to a standstill, pack ice surrounds the Greenpeace ship, "Gondwana". A giant iceberg behind and no way forward, the ship's helicopter takes to the air to search out a path. The crew feared they would be locked in for winter, but broke free into clear water after four hours.

"This [Antarctica] is the only continent left on Earth that can remind people how clean the planet should be."

Kevin Conaglen,
a Greenpeace volunteer, who over-wintered in Antarctica, 1987/88.

Lucky escape

The Greenpeace ship was lucky to escape being crushed and, despite doubts among some in the organization, the crew were undeterred and went back again the following year to continue their campaign. This time they were luckier and managed to get through the ice that had trapped them before, and made landfall at Ross Island.

Here they set up their base next to Captain Scott's famous hut. The idea was that every year four volunteers would be left to over-winter in a cabin. Each had their own tiny room with a bunk and shared meals in a large room that also had comfortable chairs. It was a recreation room with many books and videos, but only a tiny window to avoid losing heat. During the middle of their long winter, the team faced three months of complete darkness. They carried out scientific experiments and collected data for universities. They also monitored the activities of other bases in the area. Each year, the ship had to collect the old team and bring a new one.

As the organization expanded internationally, a new, more powerful boat, the *Gondwana,* was purchased in 1988. This had been built specially strengthened to force its way through the ice in the Baltic Sea as an oil rig supply vessel, and was, therefore, ideal for the Antarctic, too.

"Our job is to be outsiders, not to compromise, but to tell governments and industry to stop polluting our world. We are called a pressure group, that means putting pressure on people to clean up, and not accept any excuses. That does not make us popular but we are used to that."

Peter Melchett,
Director of Greenpeace,
November 1992.

Penguin colonies blown up

This 1988-89 trip took place during a critical year for the Antarctic. The thirty-nine nations with interests in the area had finally agreed a new treaty that would allow mineral prospecting to start. Some countries were already looking for oil. Greenpeace stepped up its campaigning worldwide and decided to take a more determined stance than ever.

The new ship, with its two helicopters and five small boats, went to visit the French base at Dumont d'Urville, due south of Australia. Here, the campaigners discovered the French were building an airstrip big enough to land giant transport planes. In order to do this difficult work in frozen conditions, the construction workers were blowing up penguin colonies on a string of islands. They were going to push the rubble from the islands into the sea to make a runway. The project involved destroying the nests of *thirty thousand* penguins.

The French said the airstrip was needed to bring in equipment for a new scientific station, but Greenpeace members, shocked by this wanton destruction of wildlife, did not believe them. They suspected the French were preparing to fly in heavy mining machinery to start mineral working on the continent.

The crew of the *Gondwana* decided to stop them. In the first action of its kind ever undertaken in Antarctica, the volunteers occupied the airstrip.

"The protesters were knocked to the ground and forcibly dragged out of the way, receiving black eyes, cuts and bruises in the process."

John May,
from "The Greenpeace
Book of Antarctica".

A million people

Despite temperatures below freezing and the angry French workers, the crew of the *Gondwana* refused to budge. Pictures of the demonstration were flashed around the world via satellite. French construction workers, worried about losing wages, brought in machines to move the human barricade, but every time they did so, Greenpeace members returned to the runway with renewed determination.

Disarray - French construction workers drag Greenpeace protesters from the paths of their bulldozers as the campaigners try to prevent the building of the airstrip at the Dumont d'Urville base, in Antarctica.

Back in France, and around the rest of the world, the ten-day battle between Greenpeace and the old enemy, France, made headlines again. For the first time, public opinion about Antarctica began to change. The famous French naturalist and underwater film expert, Jacques-Yves Cousteau, collected signatures to save Antarctica. As a result, more than a million people petitioned the French government to change policy and support a ban on mining in Antarctica.

Stiff with cold

The *Gondwana* eventually had to leave the French base and move on to re-equip the Greenpeace base at Ross Island. But on the way, crossing thousands of square miles of ice-strewn and supposedly-empty ocean, it made an unexpected find. It came across a Japanese factory ship and a fleet of harpoon boats killing whales.

The campaigners could not let pass the opportunity to publicize what they considered to be the illegal, commercial whaling activities of the Japanese. They immediately gave chase to the factory ship. Despite a three-day race through stormy conditions which, at one point, led to water pouring through the *Gondwana*'s ventilation system and putting all the lights out, the factory ship did not escape.

The Japanese then decided to tough it out and resumed hunting for whales. The *Gondwana* lowered its fast rubber boats and volunteers chased the harpoon boats through the icebergs. Time and time again, they risked their lives to get between the harpoons and the whales as the Japanese prepared to move in for the kill. Stiff from the cold, the volunteers had to be hauled aboard the *Gondwana* and be replaced by others. The battle went on for several days.

The bravery of the Greenpeace crew and a collision between a harpoon boat and the *Gondwana* ensured worldwide coverage for Greenpeace. A number of nations, which were members of the International Whaling Commission, signed a resolution demanding the Japanese stop the whale hunt. Both Greenpeace campaigns to save Antarctica and the whales from commercial exploitation were given a big boost and thousands more people joined the organization.

Russian sailors (below), involved in arresting the Greenpeace ship, "Solo", when it protested about nuclear dumping in the Kara Sea in the Arctic, take time out to read a campaign magazine.

Bottom: Before the Earth Summit in Brazil, Greenpeace drew attention to the damage that was being done to the environment by this paper pulp exporter at the port of Vitoria in the north of the country.

A World Park

One of the places where the Antarctic campaign was having a profound effect was Australia. The government accepted that in its vast empty deserts, Australia had large, unexploited mineral resources. There are enough resources in Australia for the people never to need to mine in Antarctica. To Greenpeace's delight, in the summer of 1989, the Australian prime minister, Bob Hawke, became the first national leader to support the idea of a World Park. He declared that his country would refuse to ratify the new agreement to allow mining in Antarctica and would do everything to oppose it. Then France joined Australia. For the first time, Greenpeace and France were as one.

Lots of other countries did not agree. Britain and the United States still wanted to keep the mining option open. For three years, a tense, diplomatic battle raged. Greenpeace was joined by other powerful pressure groups, like the World Wide Fund for Nature, and more and more countries converted to the cause.

Finally, on October 4, 1991, the eight-year Greenpeace battle was finally won. Twenty-two Antarctic Treaty nations signed an agreement banning mining in the continent for the next fifty years.

It was the greatest single victory the environment movement had achieved.

New members, new countries

Twenty years after the first protest voyage from Canada, the organization continued to expand. By 1991, it had become an international organization with offices in thirty countries with their own staff and campaigns, each one linking to Greenpeace International headquarters in Amsterdam.

The United Nations' Earth Summit in Rio de Janeiro, Brazil in June 1992 gave the fledgling organizations in South America a significant boost. People waited in their hundreds to visit the new *Rainbow Warrior* in all the ports it visited on a goodwill tour during the summit. Greenpeace offices already open in Brazil and Argentina were joined by Guatemala and Mexico and a new one opened in Chile.

Main picture: The notorious plant at Novya Zemlya on the River Dvina, Archangel, in the far north of Russia. Greenpeace protested because the heavy pollution from this paper-making factory is so great, it damages plant and animal life over hundreds of miles, even over the country's borders as far away as Norway and Sweden.

"When the last tree is cut and the last fish killed, the last river poisoned, then you will see that you can't eat money."

A Greenpeace banner
on a factory chimney
in Germany, June 1981.

During the summer of 1992, Greenpeace carried out its first direct actions in South America. Demonstrators drew attention to the dangers of radioactivity from the nuclear power station at Zarate, Argentina. In Brazil members objected to the plantations of Australian eucalyptus trees which cause the destruction of native forests and, in turn, forces the indigenous people from their homes.

In an otherwise unspoilt spot in the South Island of New Zealand, plastic waste from a factory is dumped in the Kaikorai estuary. Greenpeace exposed this scandal in 1991, by publishing pictures of the "river of plastic".

Walking a tightrope

Greenpeace often has to develop careful tactics if the organization is to survive.

In politically unstable countries especially, staff must not be seen by local people as being interfering foreigners telling them how to run their own country.

The non-political and non-violent beliefs of the organization have to be emphasized because, in the past, Greenpeace members have been described as communist, left wing, anti-trade unionist and extremist, although none of these descriptions is true. The International Board is very keen that local organizations are run by the local people and that they make their own decisions.

A second, and even more dangerous problem, is the nature of the governments in some of the countries in which the groups now operate. Greenpeace does not support any political party and it constantly attacks the politicians in power. Campaigners demand to know why politicians make decisions without thinking about the environment. They want to know what will happen to the people, animals and plants that depend on clean

NUCLEAR = MUERTE
STOP ATUCHA
GREENPEACE

As Greenpeace expands into more countries and membership grows, campaigns become more complex and diverse. They do have a constant theme, trying to stop the destruction of the environment. A banner protest (above) at the Atucha nuclear power plant at Zarate, Argentina, where there are fears of radioactive pollution of the local community.
Left: A selection of household cleaners that are toxic, or contain nutrients that damage the environment when they are discharged from sewage works into rivers and the sea.

One of the first demonstrations in post-Communist Czechoslovakia, where there is a real fear that the old Soviet-built nuclear reactors are unsafe. Here, in 1991, anti-nuclear protesters planted five thousand crosses as a premature memorial to those who will die if the plant suffers an accident.

air, land and water to survive. So, sometimes, Greenpeace can be very unpopular with both civilian ministers and the military.

In many places in the world this kind of dissent and disagreement is protected by the right of free speech but, in South and Central America, these ideas are much less respected. As a result, Greenpeace members in some countries face prison for their protests or sometimes beatings and harassment, which places them at considerable risk.

Campaigners or terrorists?

Decisions, about how to protest and when, have to be taken carefully to prevent a sometimes violent reaction. One of the best protections these vulnerable groups have is the presence of the press and television cameras during demonstrations, and support from millions of fellow members in other countries.

Despite the risk of angry reactions from governments or the military, Greenpeace has decided it is

important to explain why members make their protests. As a result, the organization tries to have an office in every country where it attacks the government. For example, in Japan, where environmental groups do not thrive on a national scale. Some sections of Japanese society are hostile to Greenpeace because of the anti-whaling campaigns, but in many other areas the Japanese are very concerned about the problems of the environment.

Far from the killing fields of the wild animals, whose pelts are used to make fur coats, are the stores that sell them to wealthy people. Here, in New York, Greenpeace demonstrators appeal to shoppers not to support the trade that is close to wiping out some endangered species.

Russia welcomes Greenpeace

Even before the revolutions and the demolition of the Iron Curtain between East and West, Greenpeace had begun to move into the old Soviet bloc.

After the Chernobyl nuclear disaster of 1986, when a reactor caught fire and contaminated huge areas of Russia and the Ukraine, Greenpeace was allowed to open offices in Moscow. The plight of large numbers of children living in areas that had been showered in radioactive dust became such a terrible problem that

Opposite top: Further efforts to stop trade in nuclear production and waste, as campaigners stage a demonstration in Moi, Belgium, 1992.

Below: To pay for its ships, crews, scientists, campaigns and offices, Greenpeace membership fees are not enough. Here, a young member helps with a street collection. Sponsored walks and cycle rides, T-shirt and gift sales are also organized to raise money for the cause.

Greenpeace advice and help to the Russian government was welcomed.

But not all the environmental groups that were formed to protest about these things in former communist countries were what they seemed. In many states, opposition to the one party rule was not allowed. As a result, many joined environmental groups to disguise their political activities.

In many countries, civil wars and food shortages mean people have more pressing concerns than the environment. Undeterred by these problems, Greenpeace's fight for the environment continues. The organization believes that if people can have clean land, rivers and lakes they are more likely to be able to feed themselves without having to rely on food convoys from elsewhere.

Working together

Despite its many advances in the former communist countries and in South and Central America, Greenpeace is still far from being a completely global organization.

After the Gulf War in 1991, Greenpeace scientists spent months advising Saudi Arabia, Kuwait and Iran on how to deal with the pollution caused by the terrible oil fires and spills resulting from the conflict – but there are still no offices in the Middle East. China and most of Africa are still without representation, too. The international directors believe the organization should expand slowly helping the newer organizations to build up, so there are enough members in each country to be self-supporting.

But, just as environmental problems, like global warming, affect everyone in the world, so it seems likely that many more people in different countries will become involved in protecting the environment. For example, Britain and Brazil may not seem to have much in common, but new links are already being forged between European and South American members of Greenpeace. The tropical forests of Brazil are being cut down to provide wood for houses and furniture in Europe. Some of the trees being used for this trade are so rare they are protected by law. To stop the illegal

Left: During the height of the Gulf War in the Middle East in 1991, Japanese Greenpeace plead for an end to the fighting which caused terrible oil fires and massive environmental damage.

In June 1992, the leaders of more than one hundred nations met in Rio de Janeiro, in Brazil, and promised to try and halt the destruction of the environment and repair damage already done. Greenpeace joined hundreds of other groups at the Earth Summit, where, at the opening ceremony, thousands of candles were lit as a symbol of hope for the world.

trade, the Brazilian members are joining forces with those in England, Germany and France to trace the shipments, and to catch and expose the exporters and importers. That way the public and the police in Europe can act with those in Brazil to stop the trade, and no one can pretend they did not know it was happening.

It is these links between members from different countries working together that Greenpeace believes will win the day for the environment. The organization has already seen some great successes in stopping nuclear tests, commercial whaling and nuclear dumping at sea. The Antarctic has been saved from mining for at least fifty years. As the director of Greenpeace UK, Peter Melchett, said, "We take heart from these achievements. We still see ourselves as modern Warriors of the Rainbow, fighting battles to win clean earth, air and water for all to share. From a few people going out in a small boat to protest about nuclear testing we now have a whole fleet in action and nearly five million members worldwide all working together for the same cause."

Important Dates

1970   The "Don't Make a Wave Committee" is formed in protest against US nuclear testing on the island of Amchitka.

1971   The movement is renamed "Greenpeace" by Bill Darnell, a Canadian social worker and member of the group.
Sept 15: The first protest voyage is made from Vancouver to Amchitka Island by the *Phyllis Cormack*.
Oct 22: A second protest voyage is made to Amchitka by *Greenpeace Too*.

1972   The United States announces an end to nuclear testing at Amchitka after a huge public outcry.
Apr 30: The *Vega*, with David McTaggart and a crew of two on board, leaves New Zealand to protest against the French nuclear tests on Moruroa in the Pacific.
July 1: A French minesweeper rams the *Vega* in the test zone. McTaggart begins a battle to get compensation from France.

1973   June: The *Vega* is repaired and sails again for Moruroa.
Aug 15: The *Vega* is seized by the French authorities and two of the crew are beaten up by French marines. Ann-Marie Horne smuggles out pictures of the beating as evidence.

1974   Sept 24: France announces that all future nuclear tests will be held underground.

1975   Greenpeace opens an office in Vancouver.
Apr 27: The *Phyllis Cormack* and *Vega* set sail from Vancouver as the first expedition against whaling is launched.
June 17: McTaggart wins his legal case against France; the French navy is condemned for dangerous conduct and ordered to pay compensation.

1976   Mar 2: Greenpeace launches its first expedition to save seals in the Canadian Arctic.

1977   Greenpeace UK is founded in London.
Greenpeace Europe is formed.

1978   Feb: The ship *Sir William Hardy* is bought, cleaned up in London's docks and renamed the *Rainbow Warrior*.
June: Greenpeace stages a campaign to stop nuclear dumping at sea against the British ship, the *Gem*.
Oct: The *Rainbow Warrior* challenges the seal cull off the Orkney Islands. The British government stops the culling because of "widespread public concern".

1979   The new umbrella organization, Greenpeace International, is founded, with David McTaggart as chairman.

1981   Oct: The *Vega* stages a third protest voyage from New Zealand to Moruroa, in the continued campaign against nuclear testing.

1982   Oct: The *Vega* sails on the fourth protest to Moruroa, in response to the French government's plan to strengthen its nuclear tests.

1983   Jan: Norway announces that it will cease the killing of seal pups.

1984   Greenpeace campaigns are launched to save the Antarctic and to oppose the dumping of toxic waste at sea.

1985   May 17: The *Rainbow Warrior* embarks on a "mission of mercy", to evacuate the island of Rongelap in the Pacific.

July 10: The *Rainbow Warrior* is sunk by French agents in New Zealand as it prepares to set sail for Moruroa.
A ban on whaling is imposed by the International Whaling Commission.
The annual dump of radioactive waste at sea in Europe is abandoned.
Greenpeace's membership reaches one million.

1986   The Greenpeace Antarctic base camp is established.

1989   An International Campaign to clean up the North Sea begins.
The new *Rainbow Warrior* is launched.
Greenpeace membership reaches four million.

1990   Greenpeace campaigns begin to draw attention to the danger of global warming.
The *Rainbow Warrior* is involved in action against the use of drift-nets in the Pacific.

1991   Oct 4: The Antarctic is saved from mining for at least fifty years.

1992   The United States, Russia and France halt nuclear tests.
June: The Earth Summit is held in Brazil to discuss world wide conservation issues.

1993   Greenpeace begins a new tour of Antarctic bases.
May: The International Whaling Commission is put under pressure to end the ban on minke whaling. Conservationists fear it could lead to other whale species being hunted – including endangered species, such as the blue whale.

Further Information

If you would like to find out more about Greenpeace, or how to join the group nearest to you, contact the main organization in your country.

Australia
Greenpeace Australia
Studio 14, 37 Nicholson Street
Balmain, NSW 2041, Australia,
Phone 61 (2) 555 70 44

Canada
Greenpeace Canada
185 Spandina Avenue, 6th Floor,
Toronto, Ontario M5T 2C6, Canada
Phone 1 (416) 345 8408

Ireland
Greenpeace Ireland
44 Upper Mount Street,
Dublin 2, Eire
Phone 353 (1) 61 98 36

Greenpeace International
Stichting Greenpeace Council
Keizergracht 176,
1016 D.W. Amsterdam, Netherlands
Phone 31 (20) 523 65 55

New Zealand
Greenpeace New Zealand
Private Bag, Wellesley Street Post Office,
Auckland, New Zealand
Phone 64 (9) 77 61 28

United Kingdom
Greenpeace United Kingdom
Canonbury Villas, Islington,
London, N1 2PN, UK
Phone 44 (1) 354 5100

USA
Greenpeace USA
1436 U Street,
N.W. Washington D.C. 20009, USA
Phone 1 (202) 462 11 77

Glossary

Activist: Someone who works vigorously to achieve a political or social goal.

Atoll: A ring-shaped coral reef that encloses a lagoon.

Conservation: The protection of the environment and wildlife.

Ecologist: Someone who studies living things in relation to their surroundings.

Fallout: *Radioactive* dust created by a *nuclear* explosion that can cause long-term illness.

Fuel rods: Also called fuel pins, these are long, thin tubes that are packed with *uranium,* bound into bundles and put into the core of a *nuclear* reactor.

Global warming: The warming of the earth's atmosphere, caused by a build-up of gases, in particular carbon dioxide. The layer of gases stops the earth losing heat, making it hotter.

Injunction: A court order that prevents a person from doing a specific act.

Lobby: To put pressure on those in power in order to influence a change in the law.

Neutron bomb: A *nuclear* bomb that kills people and animals by intense *radiation,* but leaves buildings in tact.

Non-violent direct action: A method of peaceful campaigning aimed at drawing attention to a problem, in the hope of creating public pressure to help the cause. Violence must never be used.

Nuclear: Concerned with the structure of atoms which give off tremendous energy when split or combined with another atom. Nuclear energy is used not only to create power, such as electricity, but also nuclear weapons.

Ozone layer: A region twelve to thirty miles above the earth's surface, which is made up from a form of oxygen. It creates a protective layer by absorbing some of the ultraviolet rays, that are given off by the sun, before they reach the earth.

Plutonium: A *radioactive* metal, manufactured in *nuclear* reactors from *uranium,* that is used for *nuclear* fuel and weapons.

Radiation: Unseen *radioactive* rays that are often caused by a *nuclear* explosion or leak. Exposure to radiation can cause vomiting, hair loss and can sometimes result in cancer.

Radioactivity: High-speed and high-powered energy, which is released spontaneously from certain atoms, in the form of alpha, beta or gamma rays. *Nuclear* explosions release large amounts of radioactivity.

Sabotage: Intentional damage, often carried out for political reasons.

Uranium: A *radioactive,* silvery-white metal used mainly for *nuclear* energy and in *nuclear* weapons.

Index